108 QUOTES

on

FAITH

Amma
(Sri Mata Amritanandamayi Devi)

108 QUOTES ON FAITH

Published by:

Mata Amritanandamayi Mission Trust
Amritapuri P.O., Kollam Dt., Kerala
INDIA 690525
Email: info@theammashop.org
Website: www.amritapuri.org

Typesetting and layout by Amrita DTP, Amritapuri

First edition: February 2014

1

The Universal Power exists within you, but this knowledge may not have taken root yet. This Supreme Truth can be attained only through faith and meditation.

2

Spirituality has nothing to do with blind faith; it is the principle of awareness that dispels darkness.

Many spiritual Masters have undertaken exhaustive research, even more than some modern scientists. While science air-conditions the outer world, spirituality air-conditions the inner world.

3

Very often we forget that strong faith and innocent love can easily walk on planes that intellect and logic fail to tread. We can see how the power of innocence has been the driving force behind the ground-breaking discoveries of many famous scientists. Have you seen how a child views everything with wide-eyed wonder? In the same way, a true scientist also views this universe with wonder. This helps the scientist probe the deepest mysteries of the universe.

4

Faith is the foundation of everything. It is the faith and devotion of people, not rituals or ceremonies, that fill temples with spiritual energy. If you have enough faith, any water can become as holy as the Ganges River, but without faith, the Ganges is nothing but ordinary water.

5

We often try to measure and evaluate life with intellectual reasoning and logic alone, but we cannot reach the depths of knowledge and experience with this attitude. We should learn to approach life's experiences with love and faith. Then life will reveal all its mysteries to us.

6

Have faith in the theory of karma (action and reaction), and you will see the invisible hands of God everywhere. The hidden power of God is the cause of all that is manifest.

7

When facts are available, there is no need for faith. It is a fact that the Earth, plants, trees, rivers and mountains all exist. Faith is not needed to know they exist. Faith is needed when rational thought fails.

Since God is invisible, to believe in a Divine existence you have to depend solely on faith.

8

Just as you trust the words of scientists who talk about facts unknown to us, have faith in the words of the great Masters who speak about the Truth; they are established in that.

9

The scriptures and the great Masters remind us that the Self, or God, is our true nature. God is not far away from us. It is who we really are, but we need faith to imbibe this truth.

10

God is not confined to a temple or to a certain place. The Divine is omnipresent, omnipotent and can assume any form. Try to behold your Beloved Deity in everything.

11

God is not a limited individual who sits alone up in the clouds on a golden throne. God is pure Consciousness that dwells within everything. Understanding this truth, learn to accept and love everyone equally.

12

The foundation of spirituality is not blind faith. It is sincere inquiry; it is an intense exploration within one's own Self. Faith in a higher power helps us to control our mind and thoughts.

Though progress can be slow and gradual, continue putting in effort with patience, faith and enthusiasm.

13

Doubting is learned while faith is inherent inside of us. Doubt is your number one enemy. Faith is your best friend. Draw it forth and learn to believe. You will then discover a positive outcome.

14

Beauty lies in faith, and faith dwells in the heart. Intellect or reasoning is necessary, but we should not let it swallow the faith in us. We should not allow the intellect to eat up our heart.

15

What we need is faith in a Supreme Power that controls the entire universe, that is beyond the mind and senses and that makes even the intellect function. We should inquire into the source of that Power, which exists within ourselves. Faith in that Cosmic Power, together with meditation to know that Supreme Power, will help us attain knowledge of the Self, unity, peace and tranquility.

16

If you want your suffering to end, pray that your desires are eliminated. Also pray that your faith and love for God grow. If you can do this, then the Divine will fulfill all your needs.

17

God is always with you and will definitely appear when you call with deep longing. Those who have the sincere attitude, 'There is no one else who can save me; You alone are my refuge,' will have all their needs taken care of directly by the Divine.

18

Some people say, 'God is just a belief,' but in truth, Divinity is within the heart of each one of us. God has no separate hands, legs, eyes, or body other than our own. The Cosmic Power inside each one of us is God.

19

It does not really matter whether you are a believer, a non-believer or a skeptic. You can be a non-believer and still lead a happy and successful life as long as you have faith in your Self and serve society.

20

Real faith is faith in one's own Self. Even if we believe in an external God, in actuality this God is inside of us; it is our own true Self.

21

Have faith in your own Self. Try to understand who you are, your true Self. That is sufficient. If you do not have faith in your Self, it is difficult to advance even if you believe in God.

22

Faith and Self-confidence are interdependent. Faith in God is to strengthen your faith in your Self, the confidence in your own true Self; this is real Self-Confidence. If this is not there, you cannot succeed in life.

23

Always remember that when dusk arrives, it's already carrying dawn in its womb. Darkness cannot remain for long. In due time, dawn will surely break out and shine. Optimism is the light of God. It is a form of grace, which allows you to look at life with greater clarity.

24

The sun doesn't need the light of a candle; God doesn't want anything from us. We are meant to use God's light to remove darkness in the world; this is the Divine principle.

25

Self-confidence gives us mental balance, courage and control over our minds. It enables us to confront the problems in our lives with courage. Some problems are inevitable and unavoidable. Having faith in yourself will help you to face and overcome them.

26

Women should never believe they are inferior to men. It is women who have given birth to every single man in this world. Take pride in this unique blessing and move forward with faith in your inherent power.

27

We are not candles that have to be lit by somebody. We are the self-effulgent sun. We are embodiments of that Supreme Consciousness, and we have to awaken to this truth. We are Love.

28

When people lose faith in God, there is no harmony or peace in society. People act and live as they like. Without faith, morality and ethics will disappear from the face of this earth, and people will be tempted to live like animals. The absence of faith, love, patience and forgiveness would make life like hell.

29

We have the capability to become whatever each of us chooses to be. We can choose to be a virtuous soul who only desires good for others in thought and deed. On the other hand, we can also choose to be the epitome of evil. The freedom of choice is the greatest blessing of this human birth, but in order to experience this blessing to its fullest potential, we should have the innocence and faith of a child.

30

Whatever religion we follow, as long as we understand spiritual principles, we can attain the ultimate goal: the realization of one's true nature.

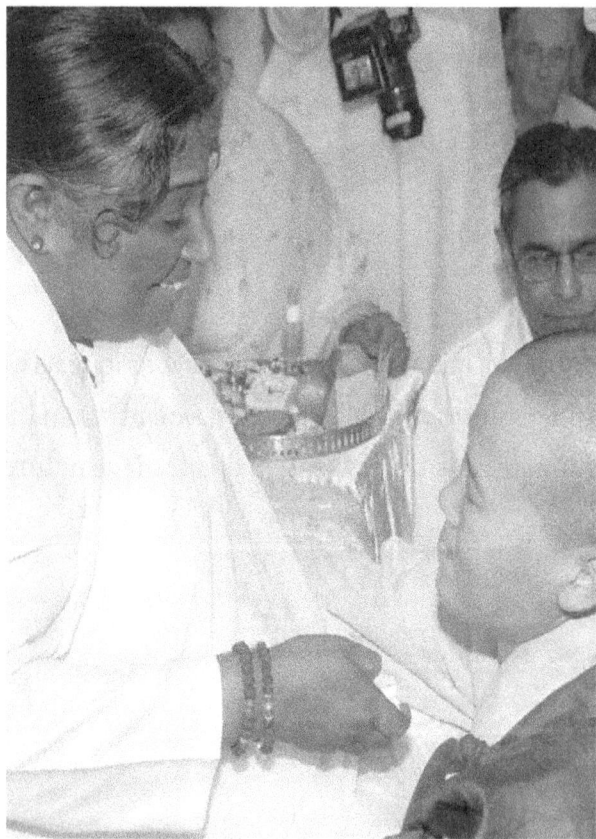

31

It is very important that we respect the feelings and the faiths of people of all religions. Faith in the immense power of the inner Self will bring true unity among people and between humanity and nature.

32

The real meaning of religion is to have faith in the existence of a Supreme Power and to live according to spiritual values.

33

There is no difference between the Creator and creation just as there is no difference between the ocean and its waves. It is the same Consciousness that pervades everything. Faith, as well as love for the entire creation, should be instilled in our children. This is possible through proper spiritual education.

34

There is no harm in having many religions and faiths, but it is harmful to think that they are different and that one faith is higher and the other one is lower. Children, do not see the differences. See the unity in them and the great ideals that they all teach.

35

Love and compassion are the underlying principles of all genuine religions. These Divine qualities are the essence of all faiths.

36

Love and faith are the cornerstones of life. Only when we serve others with the right understanding of love and faith will we ourselves be happy and peaceful.

37

Steel rods are used in construction work to reinforce concrete. Without them, buildings would collapse. Faith in God can be compared to these rods. Faith strengthens our feeble minds. If we have faith, we do not cry for illusory things nor go crazy over them.

38

The intellect is like a pair of scissors. It cuts and rejects everything and does not accept anything. The heart, on the other hand, is like a needle; it joins everything and makes seemingly diverse things one. If we dive deep enough into ourselves, we will find the one thread of universal love that ties all beings together. In this universe, it is love that binds everything together.

39

If you have true faith, then you will automatically fall into the heart. To fall into the heart is actually rising up and soaring high.

40

Faith and love are not two. They are interdependent. Without faith, we cannot love someone and vice versa. If we have complete faith and love for someone, the mere thought about that person will give us a special joy. Do we get any joy if we have no faith in him and consider him as a thief? The lover opens his heart to his beloved because he has faith in her. That faith is the foundation of love. Love springs from faith.

41

All of life rests in faith. For each step forward we need faith. Faith creates a flow, which inundates the entire universe.

42

Love is the universal remedy. When there is mutual love, attention and understanding in life, and when we have faith in each other, our problems and worries decrease.

43

Focus on love, mutual trust and faith. When you have love and faith, alertness in all of your actions will automatically follow.

44

True listening is possible when you are empty within. If you have the attitude, 'I am a beginner; I am ignorant,' then you can listen with faith and love.

45

We must have faith that God is always with us. This awareness will give us the energy and enthusiasm that we need to transcend any obstacle in life. This optimistic attitude should never leave us.

46

Children, some say there are believers who lead unhappy lives. However, true believers, those endowed with real faith, are happy and content in all situations. The sign of a true devotee is that they always have a smile of acceptance on their face.

47

Without faith, we are full of fear. Fear cripples the body and mind, paralyzing us, whereas faith opens our hearts and leads us to love.

48

When you understand the transitory nature of the world and realize the helplessness of the ego, then faith in spirituality starts to arise. The light of the Guru's grace helps us to see and remove the obstacles on our path.

49

Children, remembering that we can die at any moment will help us to have real faith and move toward God. Isn't it because there is darkness that we know the greatness of light?

50

Why place your faith in the mind? The mind is like a monkey that jumps from branch to branch, from one thought to another. It will continue to do so until its last moment. Instead, place your faith in a Master, and you will surely find peace.

51

It makes no difference to God, or to a great saint, whether or not people believe in them. They do not need our faith or our service. We are the ones who need their grace. It is only through faith that grace can flow to us.

52

The Master's sole purpose is to inspire the disciples, instilling the faith and love necessary for them to reach the goal. Creating the fire of love for God is the first and foremost task of the Master.

53

Mother does not say that you need to believe in Her or in God. It is enough to believe in yourself. Everything is within you.

54

Once you accept a Mahatma (holy person) as your Guru, strive to have innocent faith and the surrender of a child. You can get everything you need from a Satguru (true teacher). There is no need to keep searching.

55

Faith is not an intellectual process. The Master cannot be understood through the mind or intellect. Faith alone is the way.

56

Obedience to the Guru is very important. The Guru is the all-pervading Parabrahman (Absolute Self) in human form, your true Self and the underlying essence of the whole creation. Having faith in the Guru is equal to having faith in your Self.

57

Children, all of spirituality can be put into one word, and that word is shraddha. Shraddha is the unconditional faith that the disciple has in the words of the Master and in the scriptures.

58

If one has faith and obedience to the Guru coupled with knowledge of spiritual principles, vasanas (habitual tendencies) will be quickly destroyed.

59

There are innumerable instances of people who faithfully chanted a mantra and observed austerities as Amma instructed. From this, they experienced alleviation of the pain in their lives and averted calamities predicted in their horoscopes.

60

Even if a patient has the best doctor, unless the patient has faith in him, the treatment may not be effective. Like this, we must have faith in our spiritual Master. It is through this faith that we will be healed.

61

It is not enough to simply have faith in the doctor. We also have to take the medicine to get cured. Like this, you will not make spiritual progress if you simply sit back saying, 'Faith will save me,' without doing anything. Both faith and effort are required to move forward.

62

The Guru will be with you to show you the way through any struggle or crisis, but do not sit idly by just because the Guru is guiding you. Effort and perseverance are necessary on your part.

63

Both faith and effort are needed. If you plant a seed, it may sprout, but for it to grow properly, it needs water and fertilizer. Faith will make us aware of our true nature, but to experience it directly, we need to put forth effort.

64

We have to understand the limitations of our actions and the place of Divine Grace in our life. Keeping faith in that Power, my children, pray for Grace.

65

When you have complete faith, you will experience each and every object as being pervaded with Supreme Consciousness. Complete faith is liberation. When you reach this state, all of your doubts will disappear. The Guru will guide you to achieve this final state.

66

Nothing can harm a true believer. Faith can give us immense strength. All of life's obstacles, whether created by human beings or by Nature, will crumble when they hit against our firm and stable faith.

67

For a sincere seeker, spirituality is not a minor aspect of life; it is as much a part of you as your own breath. Your faith becomes unshakable

68

Faith will allow the Satguru's constant flow of grace to reach you. Mother is more than this body. She is all-pervading and omnipresent. Have faith that Mother's Self and your Self are one.

69

Once you have developed faith in a spiritual Master, do not allow your faith to be shaken. Your faith should be immovable and ceaseless. The only way your mental impurities will be eliminated is if you have complete faith in the Master.

70

Nothing can destroy the faith of sincere seekers. They will have unshakable faith in their Master and in the possibility of experiencing God and achieving the Supreme state.

71

If you have the determined faith to see every situation, both negative and positive, as a message from the Divine, then an external Guru is not necessary, but most people do not have that much strength or determination.

72

Have the firm belief that no one can undermine your faith. If someone tries to shatter your faith, see that as a test from God and move forward with conviction.

73

Trying to revive lost faith is like trying to grow hair on a bald head. Once your faith is lost, it is extremely difficult to regain. Before accepting your Guru, observe the person carefully.

74

If you pray to Mother with innocence and faith, She will definitely help you. She is always there for you. If you fall down, She will help you up.

75

Strive to be like a child endowed with tremendous faith and patience. In order to reach the goal, our faith must be inspired with the innocence of a child.

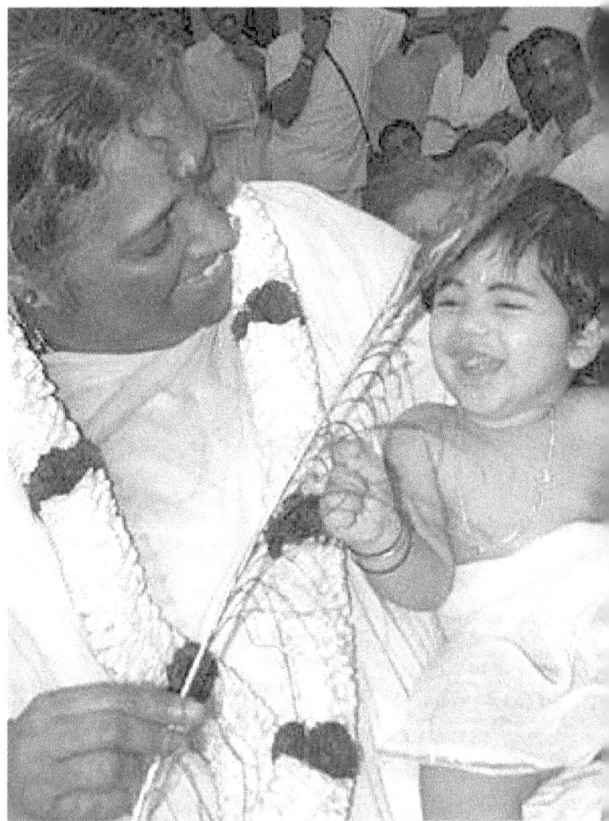

76

As we get older, we lose our enthusiasm and joy. We become dry and unhappy. Why? Because we lose our faith and innocence. Somewhere inside each of us, a child's joy, innocence and faith lie dormant. Rediscover them.

77

Play like a child. Reawaken that innocence within you. Spend time with children. They will teach you to believe, to laugh and to play. Children will help you to smile from your heart and to have a look of wonderment in your eyes. Divine love makes you innocent like a child.

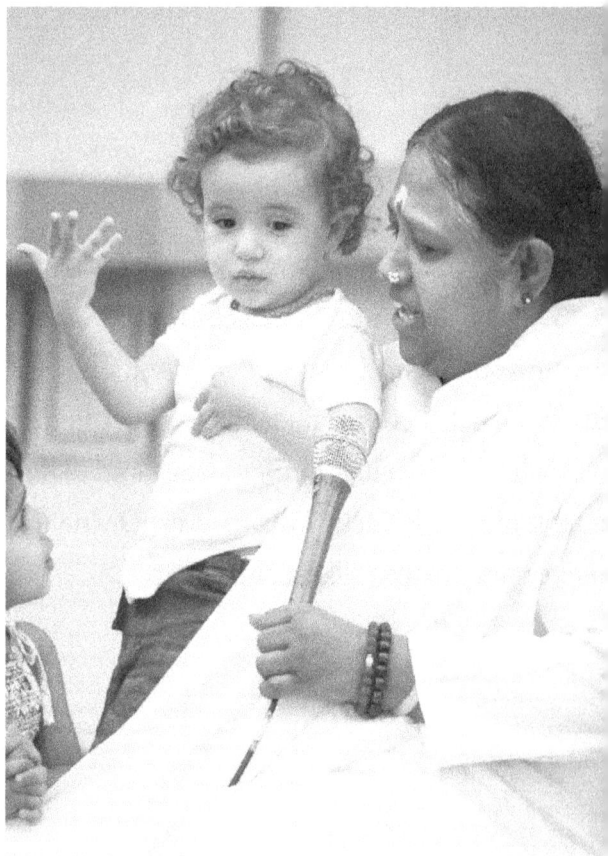

78

With the faith and trust of a child, anything is possible. Your innocence and pure heart will save you.

79

You may have to proceed little by little in spiritual development because of your samskaras (past life tendencies). It is a slow process requiring faith and confidence.

80

The spiritual energy you have acquired through your sadhana (spiritual practices) remains within you.

Keep your faith and enthusiasm. Neither your efforts nor the fruit of your actions can be destroyed. Do not ever give up hope.

81

Patience, enthusiasm and optimism, these three qualities should be the mantras of our lives. In every field, we can observe that those who have faith succeed. Those who lack faith lose their strength.

82

A person endowed with faith in the Supreme holds on to that principle when a crisis occurs. It is this faith that gives us a strong and balanced mind enabling us to confront any trying situation.

83

When you have real faith in God and practice meditation, mantra repetition and prayer, you will gain enough strength to meet any situation without faltering. You will be able to act with awareness even if the circumstances are difficult.

84

Faith in God will give you the mental strength that you need to confront all problems in life. Faith in the existence of God will protect you; it makes you feel safe and protected from all the negative influences of the world.

85

If you try to run away from your shadow, you will simply collapse due to exhaustion. Instead, face the difficulties of life through love and faith. Remember that you are never alone on this journey. The Divine is always with you. Allow Her to hold your hand.

86

A true sadhak (spiritual seeker) believes more in the present than in the future. When we put our faith in the present moment, all of our energy will be manifested here and now. Surrender to the present moment.

87

The past is a wound. If you scratch the wound by delving into your memories, the wound will get infected. Do not do that, or it will get bigger. Instead, let it heal. Healing is possible only through faith and love of the Divine.

88

We should develop faith in ourselves instead of leaning on others for solace. Only then will we find true comfort and satisfaction.

89

People and objects that you are attached to will leave you one day. Each time something or someone disappears from your life, you may be overcome by agony and fear. This will continue until you surrender to God and develop faith in the eternal nature of your real Self.

90

You are able to move and to act only because of the Almighty's grace and power. Have the conviction that God is your only true relative and friend.

If you surrender, the Divine will always guide you. With faith in that Divinity, you will never falter.

91

All your problems arise because you don't stand firm within your Self. Consciousness is the eternal source of power. This little world of ours should evolve until it becomes the whole universe. As it grows, we can see our problems slowly dissolving away.

92

Your strongest relationship should be with the Divine. Tell Her all your sorrows, and it will bring you closer. She cannot sit silent and unmoved when somebody calls with an innocent heart. Faith and surrender removes all sorrows.

93

Each of us carries a burden of sorrow and pain from past experiences. The cure is to develop love, compassion and reverence. This will heal all wounds.

94

Compassion is an extension of the faith and awareness that Divinity is all-pervading.

Those who lack compassion and are not concerned about the welfare of others also lack faith.

95

Receptivity is the power to believe, to have faith and to accept love. It is the power to prevent doubt from entering your mind.

96

Like any other decision, happiness is also a decision. Make a firm resolve, 'No matter what happens, I will be happy. Knowing God is with me I will be courageous.' Without losing self-confidence, move forward.

97

 $\mathbf{M}$ y child, never lose courage. Never lose your trust in God or in life. Always be optimistic no matter what situation you find yourself in. Anything can be accomplished with faith and courage.

98

Like nectar in the fresh morning flower, let goodness fill you. When you open up, you will find that the sun was always shining and the wind was always blowing, carrying the sweet fragrance of Divinity. There are no conditions and no force being used. Just allow the door of your heart to open; it was never locked.

99

The training and discipline that are given in youth will create a strong impression in the mind and play a great role in the building of character. Parents should take care not only to feed and fulfil the wishes of their children but also to discipline them, instilling faith and good culture.

100

If you have true faith in God, then you cannot harm Nature. This is because true faith shows us that Nature is Divine and not separate from our own Self.

101

Move forward with faith. One who has un conditional faith will never swerve from the path

102

A person who is endowed with real faith will be steadfast. A person who has true religion can find peace. The source of this peace is the heart, not the head. A belief obtained through telling, hearing and reading will not last long, whereas the faith gained from experience will last forever.

103

Where there is love, there is no effort. Drop all your regrets of the past and relax. Relaxation will help you gain more strength and vitality. Relaxation is a technique through which you can catch a glimpse of your true nature, the infinite source of your existence. It is the art of making your mind still.

Once you learn this art, everything happens spontaneously and effortlessly.

104

All actions bear fruit. The future is the fruit, but don't worry about the future. Wait patiently, dwelling in the present, performing your actions with concentration and love. When you can live in each moment of action, good results must come. If actions are performed sincerely and wholeheartedly, they must bear good fruit. Instead, if you worry about the fruit, not only will you fail to put forth the necessary effort, but you will not get the expected result either.

105

When you see life and all that life brings as a precious gift, you will be able to say, 'Yes' to everything. 'Yes' is acceptance. Where there is acceptance, the river of life will always carry you. Love simply flows. Whoever is willing to take the plunge and dive in will be accepted as they are.

106

Have faith, my children. There is no need to be afraid. Know that Mother is always with you.

107

Strong determination and unwavering faith are the two factors needed for success in everything. Have complete faith in the Almighty. Faith can create miracles.

108

Light the lamp of love and faith within you and move forward. When we take each step with good thoughts and a smiling face, all goodness will come to you and fill your being. Then God cannot possibly stay away from you. Divinity will embrace you.

Book Catalog
By Author

Sri Mata Amritanandamayi Devi
108 Quotes On Faith
108 Quotes On Love
Compassion, The Only Way To Peace:
    Paris Speech
Cultivating Strength And Vitality
Living In Harmony
May Peace And Happiness Prevail:
    Barcelona Speech
May Your Hearts Blossom:
    Chicago Speech
Practice Spiritual Values And Save The
    World: Delhi Speech
The Awakening Of Universal
    Motherhood: Geneva Speech
The Eternal Truth
The Infinite Potential Of Women:
    Jaipur Speech
Understanding And Collaboration
    Between Religions
Unity Is Peace: Interfaith Speech

Swami Amritaswarupananda Puri
Ammachi: A Biography
Awaken Children, Volumes 1-9
From Amma's Heart
Mother Of Sweet Bliss
The Color Of Rainbow

Swami Jnanamritananda Puri
Eternal Wisdom, Volumes 1-2

Swami Paramatmananda Puri
On The Road To Freedom Volumes 1-2
Talks, Volumes 1-6

Swami Purnamritananda Puri
Unforgettable Memories

Swami Ramakrishnananda Puri
Eye Of Wisdom
Racing Along The Razor's Edge
Secret Of Inner Peace
The Blessed Life
The Timeless Path
Ultimate Success

Swamini Krishnamrita Prana
Love Is The Answer
Sacred Journey
The Fragrance Of Pure Love
Torrential Love

M.A. Center Publications
1,000 Names Commentary
Archana Book (Large)
Archana Book (Small)
Being With Amma
Bhagavad Gita
Bhajanamritam, Volumes 1-6
Embracing The World
For My Children
Immortal Light
Lead Us To Purity
Lead Us To The Light
Man And Nature
My First Darshan
Puja: The Process Of Ritualistic
    Worship
Sri Lalitha Trishati Stotram

Amma's Websites

AMRITAPURI—Amma's Home Page
Teachings, Activities, Ashram Life, eServices, Yatra, Blogs and News
http://www.amritapuri.org

AMMA (Mata Amritanandamayi)
About Amma, Meeting Amma, Global Charities, Groups and Activities and Teachings
http://www.amma.org

EMBRACING THE WORLD®
Basic Needs, Emergencies, Environment, Research and News
http://www.embracingtheworld.org

AMRITA UNIVERSITY
About, Admissions, Campuses, Academics, Research, Global and News
http://www.amrita.edu

THE AMMA SHOP—Embracing the World® Books & Gifts Shop
Blog, Books, Complete Body, Home & Gifts, Jewelry, Music and Worship
http://www.theammashop.org

IAM—Integrated Amrita Meditation Technique®
Meditation Taught Free of Charge to the Public, Students, Prisoners and Military
http://www.amma.org/groups/north-america/projects/iam-meditation-classes

AMRITA PUJA
Types and Benefits of Pujas, Brahmasthanam Temple, Astrology Readings, Ordering Pujas
http://www.amritapuja.org

GREENFRIENDS
Growing Plants, Building Sustainable Environments, Education and Community Building
http://www.amma.org/groups/north-america/projects/green-friends

FACEBOOK
This is the Official Facebook Page to Connect with Amma
https://www.facebook.com/MataAmritanandamayi

DONATION PAGE
Please Help Support Amma's Charities Here:
http://www.amma.org/donations

www.ingramcontent.com/pod-product-compliance
Lightning Source LLC
Chambersburg PA
CBHW061828040426

42447CB00012B/2874